MASCARA

Beat Face. Broken Soul.

TIFFANY BETHEA & NATIMA SHEREE

Published by: Magenta Edutainment

ISBN-10: 0-692-77923-X

ISBN-13: 978-0- 692-77923-1

Printed in the United States of America

First Edition

Special discounts are available on bulk quantity purchases by organizations, associations and special interest groups.

For details please email: info@watchmagenta.com

This book is dedicated to all of the beautiful girls walking around with beat faces and broken souls. I am you and you are me. We are one and the same. I love you and am writing this book for you to find the inner beauty that I did.

TABLE OF CONTENTS

SECTION I:
IDENTITY

Self-Discovery

CHAPTER ONE

Highlighting

& Contouring

Dear Sister,

I want you to walk over to the mirror and gaze into it. You're wondering. "Is this really necessary?" Yes! What do you see? Who is looking back at you? How does she appear to you? What do you think of her? Whether you realize it or not, what you think of what you see is in direct relation to your life and exactly the way it is at this moment. It affects how happy you are on a daily basis. It impacts the relationships that are present, or not present, and how healthy they are. It drives the quality of life that you experience and so much more. Are you even aware of what you think of the woman you see? I hope that you are still looking in the mirror as you reflect on these questions.

We live in a rushed, fast-paced culture that often doesn't encourage or allow us to just stop and reflect. However, in this moment, as we attempt to dive into the core of who you are, I want you to just stop and stare. For some of you, my sisters, tears may be welling up in your eyes as you read these words, because you are realizing that you don't really like the person looking back at you. For some, there is another emotion rising; you are realizing that there is a stranger staring back at you. You don't really recognize this person. She looks like you, but you don't really know much about her. Yes, you have lived with her for quite some time, but you don't really know the soul of who she is beyond the surface. Who is she? Why was she created? What is her significance? What will be her legacy?

When I turn on the television, listen to the radio, or just observe life, I sincerely feel for my sisters who are coming of age in this present culture. There are so many messages that bombard our senses on a daily basis; most of them subtle yet deeply impactful. Every day, the average woman takes in repeated messages about her appearance, worth and virtue without even being aware of it. In a culture obsessed with image, we are constantly fed a standard that we should assume if we want to be accepted and valuable. We are told what makes us beautiful. Images of flawless models surround us every day. We see them everywhere, from the television shows we love and the commercials we must endure, to the billboards we see as we drive and the magazines at the checkout that stare back at us while we wait to purchase groceries. These airbrushed and electronically manipulated images tell our subconscious that in order to be considered beautiful and be desired, we must look like the model in the picture, even if in reality she doesn't exist.

I sincerely believe that something in us knows that the images around us aren't realistic, yet we still try relentlessly to reach these standards of beauty. Why? What drives us to chase such pipe-dreams? Is it because our male counterparts are viewing them as well? The standard of beauty for both genders is being arbitrarily shaped, and somehow, maybe we buy into the idea that in order to attract love we must look like these fantasy images. Can I tell you something, my sister? I believe it is much deeper. I believe that for many of us, it has become easier to decorate our exteriors in an effort to *portray* the image of who we want to be, rather than to actually *become* her. The images that we are fed only confirm the insecurities and doubts that we have about our own value. They exploit our inner wounds and voids, and tell us that in order to fill the hurt or empty spaces we just need the baddest weave with the best Brazilian hair around. They tell us that we need our face perfectly beat to the gods with the latest in makeup trends. They tell us that we must have the trendiest clothes, shoes and accessories. They distract us from the real core of who were are, the soul of the woman, and ensure that we decorate the outside just so.

Women in the United States are spending record amounts of money, $7 billion annually, on cosmetics and surgical procedures. [1] Money spent on cosmetic surgery and non-surgical aesthetic procedures is drastically increasing, especially among young women. 11.7 million cosmetic surgical and non-surgical procedures were performed in 2007;

---

[1] Hoovers.com. "Cosmetics, Beauty Supply and Perfume Stores Industry Overview." http://www.hoovers.com/cosmetics,-beauty-supply,-and-perfume-stores/--ID__294--/ free-ind-fr-profile-basic.xhtml

that is an increase of almost 500% in ten years. [2] Young women are increasingly showing an interest in cosmetic surgery. According to a recent survey, young women aged 18-24 had the highest approval rating for cosmetic surgery, with some 69% in favor of genetically altering their bodies.[3] And not *only* are women stretching their wallets to achieve perfection, but they are *also* risking their health to do so. According to a study of women aged 25-45, 67% are working to lose weight despite 53% having been found to be at a favorable weight for their body type. [4] 13% of women actually *smoke* to lose weight.[5] Doesn't that seem crazy? There are women who actually desire to lose weight so badly that they put their lungs and total health at risk. Has it gotten this serious? Nearly 10 million women suffer from an eating disorder and more than 80% of women reportedly are

---

[2] The American Society for Aesthetic Surgery. "Cosmetic Plastic Surgery Research: Statistics and Trends for 2001-2006." http://www.cosmeticplasticsurgerystatistics. com/statistics.html#2007-NEWS

[3] The American Society for Aesthetic Surgery. "New Study Suggests Young Adults More Approving of Cosmetic Surgery." http://www.surgery.org/public/consumer/ trends/new_study_suggests_young_adults_more_approving_of_cosmetic_surgery

[4] "Disordered Eating Is Widespread among U.S. Women."Online Survey by SELF magazine in partnership with the University of North Carolina at Chapel Hill. 2008.U.S. Department of Health & Human Services. National Women's Health Information Center. http://www.womenshealth.gov/news/english/614866.htm

[5] "Disordered Eating Is Widespread among U.S. Women." Online Survey by SELF magazine in partnership with the University of North Carolina at Chapel Hill. 2008.U.S. Department of Health & Human Services. National Women's Health Information Center. http://www.womenshealth.gov/news/english/614866.htm (online poll of more than 4,000 women between the ages of 25 and 45)

dissatisfied with their appearance.[6] 40% of newly diagnosed cases of eating disorders are in girls 15-19 years old, however, symptoms can occur as young as 5 years old.[7] Over 50% of teenage girls cite using unhealthy weight control behaviors such as skipping meals, smoking, vomiting and taking laxatives.[8]

Is it safe to say that we have a problem? We have a silent crisis that worsens daily. Isn't it time we address it? What is the real issue? Wherein lies the solution? Remember that mirror that I had you look in? What if I told you that the beginning of the solution rested there? What if that simple piece of glass could help to rescue an entire generation of young women looking for self-worth and value in the makeup aisle? What if it could help save forthcoming generations? *What if?*

The result, as you can imagine, is a group of young women fixated on outer beauty, who are willing to go to much greater lengths than previous generations to achieve their ideal look. The consequence is that girls younger than

---

[6] National Eating Disorders Association Fact Sheet (May 2008).
http://www.nationaleatingdisorders.org/uploads/file/in-the-news/NEDA-In-the-News-Fact-Sheet.pdf

[7] National Eating Disorders Association Fact Sheet (May 2008).
http://www.nationaleatingdisorders.org/uploads/file/in-the-news/NEDA-In-the-News-Fact-Sheet.pdf

[8] National Eating Disorders Association Fact Sheet (May 2008).
http://www.nationaleatingdisorders.org/uploads/file/in-the-news/NEDA-In-the-News-Fact-Sheet.pdf

ever are focused on their appearance rather than their virtue and character. The sad reality is that young women are literally *killing themselves* for beauty and acceptance. The ultimate outcome is that we have women walking around with BEAT FACES and BROKEN SOULS.

In the process of writing this book we interviewed numerous women to gain some additional perspective, and to put real lives and faces to the many statistics that we gathered. We will share their stories anonymously with you throughout. When you see an italicized comment such as this one:

"Test comment here."

...it is a quote taken directly from one of the courageous women who shared their stories with us.

I must be honest with you; when God gave us the vision to write this book, we were so excited that we immediately began putting it together, but it wasn't until we began reaching out and talking with the interviewees that I realized just how serious a topic it would be. Even after gathering the aforementioned statistics and realizing that we had a much greater problem than we initially thought, it wasn't until I put faces to those numbers that my emotions were drawn to a deeper place. Several of the interviews left me in tears, albeit happy ones; these women had endured so much, and they were grateful that I was working to preserve and share their stories with the world.

I believe you will relate and connect to the stories you're about to hear. I believe that, collectively, sister-to-sister, hand-in-hand, healing is present, and the time for full healing and wholeness is NOW!

CHAPTER TWO

Haute Couture

Chaos

Dear Sister,

In order for the massive exploitation of beauty to be effective, there must be something inside that is susceptible to it. There is some hook inside of us that makes us believe the lies that we aren't beautiful enough, and that the answer awaits us at the beauty counter. Have you bought into the lies? Whether you realize it or not, I am sure that you have, just like I have. I am speaking to you from a place of transparency and not judgment, because I, too, found myself being exploited and not even realizing it. I was walking around a "dressed up mess" and totally unaware. My hair was always salon fresh. My face was always flawless and beat to life, whether it be a natural day look or a smokey night look. I was rocking it effortlessly. My clothes were stylish, and were complimented by the perfect shoes and accessories. Now *that*, in and of itself, is not bad. I want you to understand that this message is not against beauty or looking nice. To the contrary I am a big fan of investing in oneself and looking good. I think it is important to take care of ourselves and dress for the life we want. However, the problem is, with all that exterior decoration, there is still brokenness inside that cannot be totally ignored. I could ignore the fact that I had low self-esteem, because when I was all dressed up I received attention that allowed me to pretend I was ok. The catcalls, whistles and "Hey girl, can I have your phone number?" responses allowed me to feel I was okay. I rested my worth on exterior validation and praise and as long as I looked the part.. That was until one day, when I could no longer ignore the cry that the *real* me bellowed. My soul cried from inside, constantly needing to be loved, nurtured and healed, and I just didn't notice because I looked fabulous and it felt great, temporarily.

> *"I struggled with low self-esteem for years. Because of everything I went through in my childhood, I didn't think highly of myself."*

> *"I battled low self-esteem since I was about 4 years old until early 20's. Now when I look in the mirror I can actually see beauty. I love the way I look and I feel so good about myself!"*

> *"Low self-esteem and poor self-esteem is something I struggled with very early on. I'm talking elementary school. I was one of the only lighter skinned females in my class and I was teased so badly that I wanted to my mother to give me pills to change my skin."*

Above are just a few of the comments shared in my conversations. The responses, though worded differently, were unanimous. Each of the participants struggled with self-esteem, and many of them noted that the struggle began around elementary school. All of the women being "millennials" were brought up in a time where cosmetic surgery was something that was mainly for celebrities and wealthy women. I shudder to think what their experience would be coming of age now. Would they be a part of the growing statistic of young women so unhappy with themselves they attempt to alter their appearance?

Each of the women I talked with eventually overcame their struggles with poor self-esteem. But my question is: what happens to all of the little girls with poor self-esteem who *don't* overcome it? Is it something that just autocorrects, or does it stay with them? One quick browse on Instagram, in particular, can answer this question. Half-dressed, overly-made-up women with skin tight clothes (or barely any at all) are some of the most popular images, and often reflect the woman who is still attempting to find acceptance, love and validation through her exterior.

I remember what it was like to be a "dressed up mess." Unknowingly, my confidence rested majorly on my outer beauty. The interesting thing I've learned over the years is that, often, when people are present at one extreme, they shift to the other extreme before settling at a healthy balance in the middle. Growing up, I had very poor self-esteem and couldn't stand my appearance. Once I began to grow some esteem and accept my looks, I unfortunately shifted to the *other* extreme, and began loving them *too* much. It was wonderful that I had started to love and appreciate myself, but the problem was that I had *only* focused on the outside.

Too many women in this generation are experiencing the same phenomenon. Several of the women I talked to discussed not liking their looks for several reasons while still struggling with esteem. One woman in particular shared with me how, in moving from one neighborhood to another in elementary school, she was suddenly the only light skinned girl in the class. Her classmates made her painfully aware of her difference in complexion. It caused so much pain that she started to hate her skin. She tried to tan but never reached her desired darkness in skin tone. One day, she saw a movie where someone had taken pills to darken their skin. She begged her mother for those pills, of course to no avail. Over the years she learned to love and accept her fair skin, and to disregard the taunting and hurtful remarks of her classmates.

Another of the ladies I talked to shared how she hated how thin she was as an adolescent. She constantly heard from family members that she need to eat more and thicken up, and she spent many years hating her physical appearance. She tried everything to gain weight but was *still* unsuccessful. To this day, she is still very petite. Though she has actually become a model, she had to learn to love and celebrate her package.

What I want to emphasize is that many of us, for a variety of reasons, start at one extreme (being poor esteem and poor self-image) and often end up swinging to the other extreme (which is an over-indulgence in our "beauty"). But what we all eventually find out is that beauty is fleeting and shallow, and it doesn't satisfy all the cravings of our soul. It doesn't bring us the fullness that inner beauty does. In the midst of the perfectly beat face, flawless hair, outfit and shoes, something is still missing. We need much more.

If you take another trip back to that mirror, you will discover the real you. Take a look. Do you see those eyes staring back at you? That is the *real you*. Those eyes are a window to the spirit and soul of who you are. The essence of your very core can be seen there. Look past your hair, down further than your beat brows and shadow, up from your lips popping with gloss, and stare directly into those eyes. Do you see her? She needs you to *discover* her, and not just *decorate* her. She needs you to learn what really makes her beautiful beyond what anyone can see. She needs you to validate her. The value you place on her will make all the difference in the world.

When we highlight and contour the face, we use different shades of makeup to accent the natural way light shapes our face. However, we can slightly alter the shape of our face in the same manner. We use cream or powder to lighten up some places and darken others until we have the desired shape. My sister, I sincerely think that for some of us, we are using concealer to lighten up the dark places in our lives and hide how we feel. We think that if we use just the right product we can make it all go away, just like concealer does to the dark spots on our skin. The problem is that the concealer wipes off at some point, and the blemish or mark we briefly covered is still there. We cannot hide behind our external beauty. The internal blemishes and marks are still there, and when we are bare they appear. We can only conceal them for so long.

I find it amazing what a little makeup can do for the face. The right swipe of powder on your face can give you cheekbones you don't really have and make your face sleeker. I have seen many before and after pictures, and have almost been tempted to wonder if it is in fact the same person. But even in those cases, at some point the powder or cream comes off, and what is left is *reality*. Our flawless appearances can temporarily make us feel like more than we are. If we are honest, though, once the hair weave comes out and the makeup is off, we don't always feel the same value and significance. Think about it: how many women do you know who absolutely will not wear their own hair, or can't leave the house without excessive makeup on? How many of us can actually feel our confidence fade without all the extra embellishments to our exterior, as if somehow the soul of who we are has actually changed?

What do I mean when I say "soul"? Let's get clear about what we mean when we are talking about the heart of who we are. Your soul houses the core of your being. Your will, your intelligence and ability to reason, your creative mind and memories, your emotions and the ability to feel and connect, are all part of the unique makeup of who you are. It is the collaborative design of these things all working together like a beautifully designed puzzle that reveals the mystery of you. And contrary to the culture that is so prevalent, it is here that your real worth lies, that your value, and even *beauty*, is formed. Beyond even your soul is your spirit. Herein lies the ability to be God-conscious and connect with your creator. The God-conscious part of us can sense things that we can't quite articulate. It is this part of us that can receive divine instruction and get in touch with our purpose, our destiny and our deeper meaning. Can I tell you something, my sister? You will be your most beautiful when you emphasize your spirit and your soul, and not just your body. You will be the most in touch with your value when you have highlighted and contoured the crevices of your soul.

This is just the beginning. We are going to take a thorough journey throughout this book. It will not be for the faint of heart, but it will be for the woman who is ready to be her absolute best. It will be for the woman who senses that there is something more to her than what the world (or even she) currently sees. It will be for the girl inside of the woman who is ready to heal, to *fully* heal. It will be for the woman who is ready to shine like a diamond from the inside out. And honestly, it will also be for the woman is not quite ready. I believe that together, my sister, we can do this. But we are going to have to be honest in order to really get there. You see, I remember what it was like to be a slave to my outer beauty. I fully remember what it was like for my confidence to be dependent upon the look of the day. I can literally remember times when I was flawless from head to toe, hair done, nails done, everything done, and the next week when everything wasn't as fresh, I wouldn't feel quite the same. I couldn't wait for the guys to see me when I was put together from head to toe, however, other times I was withdrawn, hoping no one saw me. I had to make sure that my image was kept up because it had become my cover. I was used to people knowing me for my "flawless" appearance, and it shielded them from the broken and unsure parts of myself. The image was my validation. I thought that maybe if they saw my exterior flawlessness, they would assume the same about my entire being, and that they wouldn't find out that I wasn't quite as put together inside as outside. Honestly, some people still did. Those who weren't very discerning or aware *did* assume that I was just as beautiful inside as what they could actually see. However, any amount of time spent with me would reveal that there was missing a sense of purpose, identity and value, and quite a bit of healing was needed. Just one long conversation with me would reveal that there had been a great deal of time spent on my hair, face, nails, clothes, et cetera, but that my spirit was bare and my soul broken.

What about you, my sister? Let me ask you a question: in considering the amount of time, energy and money invested in improving your exterior, is the same amount of time, energy and money invested in improving your intellect, emotions, will and purpose? I want you to really think about this. If you totaled up the money spent on all the clothes, shoes, makeup, accessories, and, let's even say your hair styling for one year, does it equal the value of how much you invest on becoming the woman you were designed to be? If you are like I was, the amounts are probably not comparable. I invested *much* more on my outer beauty than my inner beauty. It's not that I didn't see the need to improve as a person, I had just succumbed to a culture that totally focuses on image and appearance. How is it that we have gotten so consumed by our bodies that we have forgotten our spirits and our souls?

I believe that there is an incredible, remarkable person inside of you. I am going to challenge you to discover more about her. I am going to provoke you to unwrap her and take off all of the covers and distractions in an effort to really make her beautiful. So here we go, my sister. Buckle up!

CHAPTER THREE

Foundation

Flaws:

Daddy Holes & Mommy Pain

Dear Sister,

"Congratulations, it's A GIRL!" are the words that someone most likely heard upon your pending arrival to this world. Being a parent myself, I know that there was probably a mixture of excitement and anxiety. It is so amazing to think that we as humans have the power to create other humans, *however*, reflecting on our imperfections, it is a scary thought as well. Whenever I see babies born I am so excited. I stare at their beauty. I stare at the miracle that they are. I stare at their innocence. To my chagrin, I realize that that innocence will not last forever. Being surrounded by imperfect people, the child will also come to know disappointment, hurt and pain. It saddens me to think that their purity will eventually fade.

This is also our story, my sister. We came here innocent and precious baby girls, jovial, smiling, bouncing and ready to experience life. The way that we have experienced life up until this point has formed us into the women that we are today. A huge factor is how we were raised. Ideally, we had a mother and father whether married or not, who came together in a loving nurturing way to shape and guide us safely into adulthood. Unfortunately, you and I know all too well that this ideal (once commonplace) is no longer so common. Far too many of us are coming of age without the benefit of a healthy relationship with dad and mom.

"I struggled with low self-esteem as a child. I struggled with acceptance because I didn't have both parents. A child usually gets acceptance from their parents and when you don't have the people who brought you in the world accept you, you kind of feel inadequate. You're looking for the acceptance that you were supposed to be given from the number one people in your life."

THE DADDY HOLE

There is currently a national crisis of fatherlessness. Some 72 percent of black children are born out of wedlock, 36 percent of white children are without fathers, and 53 percent of Hispanic children are born outside the bonds of marriage.[9]It takes egg and sperm to create every human being, which denotes the presence of a "father", although unfortunately for too many children the presence of that father is not a given.

What's the big deal? Why is it important to have a father? So many people make it through their childhood

[9] Elder, Larry. "Gun Culture- What About the Fatherless Culture. WND Commentary. (January 16, 2013) http://www.wnd.com/2013/01/gun-culture-what-about-the-fatherless-culture/

without one, so is it really all that important? Let's look at what the numbers tell us[10]:

- Official U.S. data shows that 63 percent of youth suicides (5 times the average), 70 percent of youths in state-operated institutions (9 times the average) and 85 percent of children with behavioral disorders (20 times the average) are from fatherless homes

- Teens in single-mother households are 30 percent more likely than teens in married-mom-and-dad-families to engage in risky behavior like drinking, drugs, delinquency, and dropping out of school.

- According to the U.S. Census Bureau, children in father-absent homes are five times more likely to be poor. In 2002, 7.8 percent of children in married-couple families were living in poverty, compared to 38.4 percent of children in female-householder families.

- Teens without fathers are twice as likely to be involved in early sexual activity and seven times more likely to get pregnant as an adolescent.

- 90 percent of all homeless and runaway children are from fatherless homes – 32 times the national average

It's probably safe to say that whether we want to acknowledge it or not, fathers make a major impact in their presence or absence. As females, if we can be honest, we tend to naturally feel safer with men around. Something about a

---

[10] Growing Up Without A Father ™ Facts & Figure Page.
http://www.growingupwithoutafather.org/learned.html

man's presence brings a sense of safety, calm and security. These are the exact things that a good father will provide for his children. Children without the benefit of a father are often more vulnerable and exposed. "Girls without dads who love them unconditionally and tell them they are beautiful are especially vulnerable to the 'lines' of predators. An FBI agent asked an incarcerated sex trafficker where he found his young victims. The pimp explained, "It's easy. I see a girl at the mall. I go up to her and say, 'You have beautiful eyes.' If she smiles and says 'Thanks,' I leave her alone. But if she looks down and says, 'No, I don't,' I know I've got her."[11] Why is that? The rebuttal of the compliment indicates the presence of low self-esteem, and the low self-esteem makes her vulnerable and open. She is prey for someone who will make her "feel better" about herself.

Daddy shapes the safety, trust, security and esteem of his daughter. He affirms and validates her with his presence and the example that he sets over the course of her life. Even an imperfect dad will leave his daughter with a map or a guide with which to compare and attract healthy male interactions throughout her life. To the contrary, when dad is missing, there is a serious lack of safety, trust, security and esteem for the little girl. She can go the rest of her life looking for what

---

[11] Growing Up Without A Father ™ Facts & Figure Page.
http://www.growingupwithoutafather.org/learned.html

he was supposed to provide and what she absolutely deserves to get. For the fatherless girl, she may not even be able to articulate what is missing or how it is impacting her life, but it will be evident in her choices and interactions. The gaping hole that fatherlessness creates is not one that can be easily covered up or minimized.

The daddy void or hole tends to impacts sons and daughters differently. Fatherless sons release their pain in the form of anger and aggression. Though we are seeing a rise in violence among young women and teenage girls, the majority of fatherless daughters tend to release their pain in a much more subtle manner. Fatherless girls usually look to fill their daddy hole with sexual activity. (W*e will explore this further in chapter 4.*) They are much more likely to be promiscuous and get pregnant as an adolescent. Ironically, fatherless girls are birthing the next generation of fatherless children. For that reason alone, we must solve the crisis of hurting fatherless girls everywhere.

My sister, are you a fatherless girl? I want to tell you that IT IS NOT YOUR FAULT! It is not your fault that your dad wasn't there. He had his own pain, and as you have probably heard, hurt people hurt people. I am not sure why your daddy wasn't consistently present, but I can assure you that it was not your fault. One thing I know is that the child's perspective is undeveloped and self-centered. Maturity brings a fuller perspective. When daddy isn't there as a child, your perspective hasn't developed to the point where you can consider his pain, his relationship to your mother or any other factors. All you see is that daddy isn't there, and it feels like something *you've* done wrong. You know that in addition to what you do have, there is something else that's supposed to be there but isn't. If those wounds never properly healed, your little broken heart grew into a big broken heart that you've gotten used to over time. The disappointment has become an old frenemy. You don't like it, but it has been present so long that it is comfortable. Do you know that it is possible to be comfortable in pain? If your heart was never tended to properly, it is likely that your small distrust grew into *massive* distrust that has become a safe place. You've created a brick wall outside of your heart with a pit-bull guarding it; you won't let others in and you also can't get out. Up until now, you may not have realized that it was all because of your daddy hole.

"My relationship with my father has not always been the best. I allowed the thoughts of him from family members to become my thoughts of him. I told him I didn't need him because he didn't do anything for me when I was about 15 years old (which was not true.) I blamed him for not being there when I was being an irrational teen."

Far too often, mothers and their families taint the children's view of their father due to their relationship, making it hard for the children to establish a healthy relationship; this fact was bravely echoed by the young lady above. It perpetuates the mistrust and the emotional walls that so many women unnecessarily build. She went on to share that, in her reflection, she realized her dad always made sure she and her siblings had what they needed. He wasn't there for them physically as much as she would have desired, but he was there in some sense; he had at least tried. He was giving the best he could given the circumstances. Their relationship has grown over the years, and she has learned the true meaning of forgiveness.

"For many years, my father was like a visiting relative. When he came around, I felt like I had to compete for his attention. As I got older, I found myself doing the same thing with men. If I was 'extra special' he would stay around."

As I talked with the young woman who shared the above statement in her interview, she candidly opened up about how her unhealthy relationship with her father led to many unhealthy relationships with men, including the two fathers of her two young children. For many years, she struggled and made questionable choices. It wasn't until she had a heart to heart with her father in her early twenties that the healing began to take place, and his affirmation and validation began to replace all of the abandonment and rejection that had driven many of her decisions.

Sadly, there are countless other women with the same story. Maybe your father wasn't completely absent, but he was inconsistent. You weren't quite sure if he would show up for you, and it taught you that this is the behavior you should expect from men who love you.

There is yet another layer to this issue of fatherlessness: the physically present but emotionally absent father. For some reading this book, you had the benefit of physically consistent access to a dad, but he was not emotionally there in the way you needed him to be. You see, it is not just the physical presence of a dad that makes the difference; it is the emotional connection that truly nourishes a daughter in the deepest places, and will allow her to flourish emotionally.

Someone is reading this book right now and identifying with the daddy hole for the first time ever. Is it you? Are you the one reading this saying, "Wow, I never realized that I was physically around my dad, but the lack of emotional connection has impacted me." If it is you, I applaud you, my sister, for recognizing it. It can be much harder to identify than someone who has a clearly absent dad.

The fact that dad is present but the quality of relationship is poor is harder to notice, but it can have the same negative effects on a daughter.

"My dad was so significant in raising me, and truly raising me. Not just upbringing but truly investing in me. Which was kind of weird for me because my dad was also abusive. I didn't understand how he loved his daughter so much but not the woman who bore her. It was a struggle to understand his anger and violence toward my mother but was so opposite to me; very soft, and engaged and protective."

My conversation with the young woman above was the perfect illustration of what happens when the father is *physically* present, but not necessarily *emotionally* present. Many dads who are struggling with their own healing are present for their daughters physically, but are not modeling healthy emotions. In this situation, often times the daughter may have confidence because of the dad's physical presence, but may still struggle in her relationships with men because of the unhealthy or possibly immature emotions that she has witnessed.

I recognize that you are all totally unique and have a variety of different stories. Everyone with a daddy hole is different. I want to encourage you to examine how the daddy hole has personally impacted your life. What did you use to cope with the pain and emptiness left by an irresponsible or absent daddy? How have you tried to fill the void that you felt? Who did you become to live with the pain?

Have you ever been honest with yourself about how you feel about being a fatherless girl? As women, so many of us are taught to be strong and act as if everything is okay. Even when our heart is crying out from inside, we attempt to mask it with beauty, relationships, status, etc. But in enough time, we discover that superficial things cannot fill the space that was created for daddy. We cannot get what we need and begin our healing if we are not first honest about what we did and did not receive. I know you are drop dead gorgeous; every hair is in place and your face is beat to the Gods, my sister. But at the center of it, are you still just the little girl waiting for daddy to come and get her? Are you emotionally waiting for daddy to tell you that you are beautiful? Are you searching for someone to tell you that you are good enough, which is what daddy was supposed to tell you?

It may be impossible to turn back the clock and redo your childhood. However, I want to be the one to tell you that you can make up for what you were supposed to receive from daddy. It is not too late to get the safety, trust, security and esteem that was supposed to be given to you by your daddy. You are not a lost cause, damaged goods, too far gone or broken to the point of no fixing. You may be missing some necessary pieces to your womanhood, but they can still be yours.

The first thing that you must know is that you can drop the bags that have come with being a fatherless girl. Remember the song *"Bag Lady"* by Erykah Badu? All of us have been that bag lady at some point *"dragging all them bags like that"*, we've just had different bags. As a fatherless girl maybe your bags have been abandonment, rejection, shame, low self-esteem, insecurity, neediness and distrust. Well, it is time for you to drop those bags and walk on with your head held high queen. Seriously, you couldn't control the circumstances surrounding you as a child, nor could you control how they impacted you. I know, it wasn't fair. I understand. Now, however, you *can* control how you decide to move forward. You can choose to stay broken, or you can embrace wholeness.

"Where do I put together the pieces that I am missing?" you may be wondering. I cannot promise you that it will be an easy journey, but I *can* promise you that it is doable and that you will come out better on the other side. I want you to hold on to this thought, because we are going to revisit this in a later discussion.

MOMMY PAIN

As if it wasn't bad enough that we are experiencing an epidemic of fatherlessness in our country, one of the things that is causing it to be so devastating is the presence of hurting and distracted moms. For so many children who do have a partially or completely absent father, far too many have a mom that is devastated from the absence of dad and/or is distracted by her own wounds. This combination has left far too many children emotionally fending for themselves as they struggle to find someone to connect with and experience healthy emotions.

I will never forget a class I took; one day the topic dealt with children's attachment styles to their mothers and the connection to their personalities. The teacher shared how different levels of attachment influenced children's trust levels and confidence in people for the rest of their lives. It was in that psychology-based class that I discovered the importance of the child's relationship to the mother and how it impacted his or her relationships going forward.

Someone reading this book can relate to the pain of growing up without a healthy mommy-daughter relationship. While we are beginning to hear more about the tragedy of fatherlessness, as we should, we even more rarely hear about the pain of broken mommy-daughter relationships and how it impacts those of us with fathers and those of us without.

"Growing up my mother wasn't very supportive. She would always second guess or downplay every accomplishment. When I brought a guy home she would always ask, "What do you want with her", as if something was wrong with me. As an adult, I often heard her voice in my head."

Fighting back tears, the young woman who shared this story with me has worked hard to move beyond the toxic relationship that she still has with her mother. At one point in her journey, she had an unhealthy relationship with her dad. However, they were able to reconcile and have a great relationship. It is her mother-daughter relationship that has suffered the most and continues to confront her daily. It is her mother-daughter relationship that has caused her to second guess herself to this day. It is the words from mommy that even as an adult she is attempting to rewind and erase from her heart and mind.

As one of the young ladies shared earlier, your parents are the first people you look to for validation and acceptance, and for many, it is just as painful to have a mother who does not lend the appropriate love, support, validation, encouragement and acceptance as not having a father provide those things.

"My mother and I have a good relationship but we don't have an emotional relationship. We communicate, spend time together, talk, etc. but that is it. My grandmother never hugged my mother or told her she loves her so my mother doesn't know how to do it with me. I didn't think it affected me at all until I would see mothers hug and kiss their children of all ages. I thought to myself, "Man we've never had that!" It hurts me to the core and has taught me that I don't want to be that way with my children."

When hearing the above story, my heart was overwhelmed with compassion. It would seem so simplistic or instinctive even to show affection for those we love, but the truth is, we must be taught how to release those innermost emotions and share them with those closest to us. It is not automatic. As women we are emotional beings. Our gift to the world is embedded in our emotions and our extraordinary sense of feeling. While we are said to be much more demonstrative with our affection than our male counterparts, this story (and the countless other similar ones that I came across during interviews) illustrates the fact that without the ability to release our emotions, we may also be left with a limited emotional vocabulary.

"A daughter's first view of womanhood is immensely shaped by her mother. Despite the powerful imagery in the media and countless other images a young woman will encounter daily, not many will be more powerful than those of the woman whose bosom nourishes her." I shared this in Chapter 1 of "The Mother Daughter Journey", which I penned with my own mom. I was illustrating just how influential a mother is in the life of her daughter. The daughter, on her journey to womanhood, will collect lessons, many of which will be from her mother. She will form her own identity, some of which will be borrowed from mom, and some of which will be innately hers. It can be quite a journey navigating safely to womanhood through a mother's example; even in a healthy mother-daughter relationship there are obstacles, so it goes without saying that an unhealthy relationship comes with countless difficulties.

"My relationship with my mother as it is today did not happen until I was a grown woman. As a child I hated her. I didn't respect her. I respected her in the sense that I never put my hands on her or lashed out at her verbally or was disrespectful; but in my heart I harbored sincere hate for her. Her very presence irritated me. My mother had a drug habit and was abusive; she was a very unhappy person. She put everything before her kids. Like any man that she was dating or dealing with they came before us. And it hurt so much because when my parents divorced and my dad was out of the home and he would send money here for us, she would use it for her and to entertain her men. So we would literally be hungry and not have school clothes because she was using that money for herself."

Listening to this woman as she courageously shared her experience with her mom moved me to tears. As she was talking, my mind went immediately to the distracted mother. In this situation, the young woman's father was no longer in the home, but in reality, mom wasn't really there, either. As I continued to listen, I just heard a cycle of pain. The young woman went on to share that, before her parents' divorce, she had witnessed her father being abusive to her mother. So I had to ask myself, what was going on with mom? What would cause her to end up in an abusive relationship? What existing pain drew her there, and was then exacerbated by that relationship? What was left besides pain to give to her daughter? We often hear the phrase "Hurt people hurt people." It is such a sincere sentiment. We can only give what is inside of us. Even if we desire to give more, we simply cannot give what we do not possess.

This woman's story is so common, and I have heard it countless times. How many single mothers raising children place the men in their lives before their children, attempting to fill their own voids and creating new empty spaces in their babies' hearts? Generational pain is perpetuated. So much of the BEAT FACE BROKEN SOUL story is written by the absence of fathers and distraction of mothers. Is it worse to be completely gone, or to be present and harmful? I cannot say that I know the answer to that question. One thing I do know is that for the parent that *is* present, the emotional climate they set in the home is one that will either position us for greatness or be a major stumbling block we have to work to overcome.

As I was listening to this particular woman share how her mother would take the money their father sent and use it for herself, my heart just broke inside. I know all too well that this happens. We talk about it happening on a larger scale when celebrities and athletes are forced to pay excessively high amounts in child support. The sad reality is that it happens to everyday men, too. Can you imagine the insecurity and low self-esteem caused by not having all of your basic necessities? Conducting this particular interview, I also heard the sheer anger that it causes. This young lady knew her father was sending in money so that she could be cared for, but she never saw the benefit of it. Her heart harbored a true anger and hatred for the same woman who had given her life.

"I remember that she would bring all types of men into the house. I'm thinking to myself you have teenage daughters who are developing, who are attractive; people are crazy and you're so comfortable bringing these random men around then not concerned about our safety at all."

Shared by the same young woman we just discussed, this brought my mind to a glaring statistic: 1 in 5 girls will experience sexual abuse, most often by someone they know and trust. I wonder to myself how much this number could be improved by eliminating the distraction of mothers. How many of these people that are in the "know and trust" category are "Uncle Charlie" or whatever the play name is for mommy's current "friend"? My heart bleeds not only for the innocent daughter who should be safe but isn't, but also for a mother so entrenched in her own hurt and pain that her child's physical and/or emotional safety is left completely unguarded.

Mommy pain is real and can drive a woman to make poor decisions, which can cause struggles very similar to fatherlessness. Both parents provide for us emotionally, and when either piece is missing, it can be detrimental. As I listened to women discuss their relationships with their mothers and how it was in fact *this* parent who had done the most damage, I reflected on something I had learned. I remember one day I was in a class called "Whole Is Our Goal"; it combines psychology and personal development from a spiritual perspective to help individuals achieve true wholeness. As I mentioned earlier, the evening the instructor was teaching about attachment styles between mother and child and the results that would appear in the personality was such a memorable on. I remember this moment with such powerful clarity. I remember where I was sitting. I remember who was sitting near me. I remember where the instructor was standing. The information had hit me like a ton of bricks. I left class reflecting on my own parental relationships and that of others I knew. I remember coming to the full understanding that, just as the father-daughter relationship powerfully impacts how we as women relate to others and especially men, so does the mother-daughter relationship.

Our parents do the best they can and give us all that they have. In the end, it is up to us as we come into adulthood to sort through our childhood and decipher what we received. What went well? What didn't go so well? Did we feel abandoned, unappreciated and misunderstood? Did we receive love, nurturing, affirmation, support, affection and guidance? Were we safe, physically and emotionally? We must begin to sort through the pieces so that we can come up with an accurate assessment of what we have and what we must get ourselves. Daddy holes and mommy pain are real. But they don't have to be the end of the story. You can move beyond it. You can be better than who they were, what they did and what they gave you. It is not how or where you start, my sister, that ultimately matters. It is where you DECIDE to finish. You are bigger and better than your childhood. You are more than all the words that have been spoken over you.

You will go further than you ever imagined. You are not your past. You are your tomorrow!

CHAPTER FOUR

Running

Mascara:

Sex for the Wrong Hole

Dear Sister,

Do you know what so many of us do to attempt to fill our daddy holes and soothe our mommy pain? We try to heal them with a penis. Yes, I just said that, and I absolutely meant it. We attempt to fill our many voids and heal our many heartaches with some man's penis. That's where we are going in this chapter, so hold on and strap in; it's time to get to the raw, uncut truth.

Unplanned pregnancy and STD's are running rampant, and *still* there is so much casual sex out there. It's mind boggling. Women are constantly paying for the results of their sexual choices, and yet it hasn't seemed to change our attitudes or behaviors much regarding sex. Videos and pictures surface everyday with young women degrading themselves and performing various sexual acts in the most absurd places and settings, and all of this for what? Have you ever really stopped to consider why so much sexual looseness is prevalent? Has anyone really thought about the fact that it is about more than the pleasure that even the best orgasm provides? It is not just about the arousal or ecstasy of the moment; it is about something much deeper.

"I did not know the value of my body. I addition I didn't know how to say what I wanted and didn't want. So I would accept advances or have sex even though I didn't want to."

Too many women can relate to this sister's very honest and transparent statement. The problem with many ladies' sexual choices is not derived from being unaware; the problem is the value that they place on themselves. When women value something, they know how to treat it. They don't have to be taught how to care for something they hold in high regard. Just look at the way most women care for their exterior. I have seen women go so far out of their way not to get their hair messed up by rain, or move around very cautiously so as not to dirty the very nice outfit that they're wearing. Do you know any women who keep their shoes in the original boxes they came in to care for them? I do. I am one of them. What about women who keep their designer handbags in the original bag for protection? I know women who keep extra pairs of shoes in the car so that they do not drive in the nice ones. (Once again, I, too, am guilty of this.)

The point I am illustrating is that we as women know how to care for things that we deem precious. I shudder to think that some of us protect our cell phones and tablets better than we do our vaginas. We wouldn't let some of the people we sleep with care for our personal belongings, but we give them access to our most precious and sacred space. And why? Why do we really do it?

As the young sister said, most of us do it before we fully recognize our value or learn to speak up. And it is directly related to what we experience in childhood. If we have a history of rejection, abandonment, loneliness or loved ones not providing for us physically or emotionally, we are left with holes, voids and pains that we usually fill with some boy/man. Many times, as she shared, we don't even desire the act of sex; we just want the touch, validation or affection, and we get it in the best way that we can receive it. I myself have been guilty of engaging in sexual activity that I didn't even desire at the time, but again, it was the *perceived* affection or closeness that I really wanted. And for some reason, even though it would always end with the eventual return of the loneliness or pain, it was as if I couldn't say no. I know that, unfortunately, I am not the only one who has experienced this.

Why can't we speak up for ourselves and say no? Why can't we be assertive about what we do and don't want sexually? Often times it is rooted in rejection. We are so afraid that if we stand up for ourselves that he will walk away, so we would rather sacrifice our spirit, soul and body than to feel pain or rejection. That decision, my sister, is a huge indicator of a pain that must be thoroughly healed.

The truth of the matter is, in many of these situations the man probably *will* walk away; it's just a matter of time. Needy, open, vulnerable women tend to attract men desiring to take advantage and get all that they can from her. I believe that, deep down, we *know* this, and so we give and give and give hoping that it will keep them, but we are still eventually discarded.

I remember the relationship I had in college where, in my season of brokenness, I had attracted a complete user. He was happy and content to take and take and take. I was in a place where my esteem was growing but still fragile, and I felt like in order to keep him I had to continue to give. Keep in mind that at this time I was "flawless" in my appearance. If you had seen me at the time you would have thought for sure that my flawless hair, beat face, stylish clothes and shoes and swagged out walk meant that I was one confident sister who knew her worth, but the truth is that it was all a facade. I was beautiful outside, but ugly and scarred inside. I needed someone to tell me that I was beautiful because I wasn't sure. He told me I was beautiful, but it wasn't genuine. He said it, but not for the right reasons. It was just to get what he wanted from me. And he got it, repeatedly, because he provided me with the validation I sought and soothed pains that were present. Even though I didn't enjoy or desire it, I allowed him the pleasure of my sacred body over and over until finally one day I simply had enough.

"I remember going to the doctor at 14 and the doctor asking my mom to step out of the room. She was puzzled and looked confused. The doctor shared that at that age there is confidential information that they have to discuss with the patient. I told my mom it was okay to stay in the room with us. The doctor proceeded to tell me that I was pregnant. Immediately I saw the disappointment on her face and I knew I had made a really big mistake. I was raised in the church and I knew that we would be judged. I made the decision to have an abortion. I knew it was serious. I was faced with the consequences of my choice. "

Sometimes in the heat of the moment we sincerely forget that there can be serious, lasting consequences for our impromptu sexual choices and our attempts to soothe emotional pains with physical pleasure. Talking with this interviewee, I could hear in her voice all these years later the impact this experience still had on her. Now happily married with more children, as she reflected on this experience from her teenage years, it was clear that it is still a part of her. She was another one who candidly shared the fact that, in hindsight, it was her father's inconsistency in her life that left her starved for attention from males, and which caused early sexual activity at just 12 years old. In fact, both of her parents struggled with drug addiction, and with little supervision and stability, she was desperately in need of love, affection, belonging and approval. She found that temporary love, affection, belonging and approval in the arms of young men whose touch temporarily met her need.

The thing we have to realize is that our male counterparts deal with their own daddy holes and mommy pain. For them, of course, it plays out differently; many males struggling to find their manhood in the absence of a father or with the distraction of a mother will seek it out in some woman's vagina. In between her legs, he will attempt prove his manhood to himself and to others. And not just in between *her* legs, but as many as he can find as he seeks his own sense of value and worth.

So we must know what we are up against, because many of us are so starved for some validation or some approval that we don't take a moment to recognize if it is genuine or not. It reminds me of someone who is hungry. Have you ever been seriously hungry and then all of a sudden eaten? It was probably so delicious! You might not have been sure if the food was actually *tasty*, or whether if your hunger was simply *satisfied*. I've experienced this; I've eaten something when I was hungry and it was great, but then when I came back less hungry and tasted the food a second time, the magic was gone. Those moments are perfect illustrations for the fact that we are not great at judging quality when we are desperate.

The young girl or the mature woman who is in desperate need of daddy's validation or mommy's approval is not the best judge of whether the man in her life is sincerely *caring* for her, or is just there to get what wants because his presence is filling an emotional hunger pang.

The woman I talked with who shared her story of teenage pregnancy and abortion mentioned how she was raised in church and she knew scripture well. Her choice, however, stemmed from an emotional need that was unmet, which someone then exploited, causing her shame, disappointment and hurt.

Do you know how sex was truly designed? Do you understand the real power of what happens during sex? Let's look at sex from a biblical view. In Genesis Chapter 2, we see the beginning of the romantic and sexual relationship. Adam recognizes Eve and calls her his own. The two became one. Notice there is no mention of an actual wedding ceremony. The act of them coming together was the consummation, or what began the process of them becoming one. Many biblical references to sex discuss it within the parameters of marriage. Many people feel as though that idea is outdated and unrealistic in the modern day. However, if we dig a little deeper, we can understand why that notion is just as relevant today as ever.

It is said that when two people come together physically, they not only connect their bodies, but their *energy* is shared with one another. This is how the act of consummation comes to fruition. The husband and wife say their vows and make the promises to live their lives as one. However, it is through their bodies coming together that this act is cemented. Why? Because not only are their *bodies* entwined, but so are their *spirits and souls*. When a woman climaxes, she releases oxytocin from the brain. This very powerful hormone is only released from the brain in two instances: when she reaches sexual climax, and when she is nursing her baby. Oxytocin is also known as the "bonding hormone"; it is said to lower our natural defenses and cause us to trust more. It increases our level of empathy and allows us to bond very deeply. The problem is that our bodies can't distinguish whether the person we are engaged in sexual activity with is someone we should be developing a strong emotional attachment to, or someone who shouldn't be allowed within 50 feet of us. Science tells us that women produce more oxytocin than men do, which is why we are more likely to let down our guard and fall in love after sex. Men, on the other hand, release a simple pleasure hormone called dopamine when they reach orgasm, rather than the bonding hormone.

So we can see just from our physical makeup how powerful the act of two bodies becoming one can be. We can also see why, in the context of a loving and committed relationship, it helps to produce a bond and bind two people together. However, in a *casual* situation, it is the reason why so many of us end up feeling broken, lost and empty. Some man is walking away with a part of us that was never intended to leave that way. We can see that for the woman, the act of sex bonds and glues her emotionally to the man that she is with. But for the man, this is not the case. So if he does not already have a strong emotional attachment to the woman he is sleeping with, what happens? He can enjoy the physical act of sex, release the pleasure hormone and go on about his day without another thought for that woman, all the while she may be somewhere picking out wedding dresses and trying out her first name with his last name.

Oxytocin is pretty powerful, my sister! It has aided in tricking many people into thinking that they have great relationships because they simply have great sex. Once those hormones get going, they take over. We literally become blinded. People outside of the relationship can see the red flags, but we are so deceived by the sex that we totally miss the signs. Have you had that girlfriend that was with a guy you knew she shouldn't have been with? Hopefully you weren't that girl. More than likely, though, if you are like me, you have been her at some point. I think we have all had our turn playing the fool for someone who was completely undeserving. All of our friends and family can see that the relationship is not healthy, but they have an unfair advantage; they are not under the influence of the big O, oxytocin. When we break up and cease sexual activity, we can begin to see clearer and can ask ourselves, "What was I thinking?" The answer is: we weren't! We were on autopilot and so entranced by the penis that we couldn't think straight. And let me interject here, I'm not speaking of the quality of the sexual experience (even though that can definitely make a difference); the truth is, it doesn't even have to be great to have our minds twisted. I know I'm not the only one who has been caught up in a situation that truthfully wasn't even all that pleasing, but just the affection it provided was better than nothing. My sister, we have to be so careful, because our bodies will lie to us and keep us in completely unhealthy situations. Those hormones are mighty powerful, and regardless of the partner we have chosen to be intimate with, our bodies will do what they are designed to do. We choose temporary people to engage in permanent actions with and we can't figure out why it causes so much turmoil.

Can you see the problem now? And that is just on the physical level. What happens on a spiritual level when two people engage in sexual activity? When you look at how amazingly our bodies are designed, we must remember that our spirits are just as complex. Our bodies are just temporary houses for our spirits, so can you imagine what takes place while engaging in sex? Not only are the physical organs intertwined and connecting, but so are the spirits of the two individuals. This is why it is so necessary for us to send a balanced message when talking to our young people about engaging in safe sex. Oftentimes we discuss precautions to prevent them from contracting sexually transmitted diseases, but unfortunately, there is no condom or birth control method to prevent spiritually transmitted diseases or soul-ties. There is no (and probably will never be) a contraceptive device for the spirit.

Let's take it a step further. As women, we were created to be receivers. When we are engaged in sexual activity, our partner enters our physical bodies and we are one at that time. They release and leave a deposit inside of us. This is not only a physical release, but also a spiritual release. The more and more we engage in sex with a man, the more and more of his essence we take on. Did you know that his essence will permanently become a part of you? Research has proven that the physical essence and DNA of former partners linger in a woman's vagina, and can even become a part of her forming baby when impregnated by someone else. Isn't that scary to think? Are the men you are engaging in sexual activity with quality enough for their DNA to help shape your future children? If nothing else, does this truly illustrate the permanence of sex and the fact that it is not to be given to just anyone?

So how do we begin to make healthier sexual choices? Of course, I would say abstinence. I believe that God's way is best, and that we should wait for the person who has demonstrated that they value us the way God does, who is worthy of our precious bodies. I know, however, that the reality for some of you reading this is that that simply will not happen, and I understand, my sister. I am not here to judge, only love. To you I say we must close up our daddy holes and seek healing for our mommy pain and other wounds. Only then will we understand our value enough to choose people who will care for us the way we deserve to be cared for spiritually, emotionally and physically. Once we have addressed our rejection, abandonment and self-esteem issues, we can be picky and discerning enough to engage in sexual activity with people who are trustworthy and will not place us in harm's way.

CHAPTER FIVE

Pretty

Mugshots:

Angry Hurting Hearts

Dear Sister,

We live in a culture where black women are often labeled as "angry". It has become the plight of the black women in society to first overcome the labels, titles and stigmas unfairly placed on us. However, how do we respond and what do we do when the stereotypes are true? How do you address those who have labeled you or point out your anger issues? Take a minute and think about how you respond in certain situations; what are you facing at times that you become most angry? Do you have something in mind? Okay, now tell me, does the situation at hand truly warrant the level of anger in your response?

Oftentimes we become enraged by the smallest thing because it truly is a reflection of what we feel on the inside. Usually there is an underlying issue that has gone unaddressed, and because it still hurts you, the slightest thing can trigger that emotional response. It can literally be the smallest spark that reminds you of an incident or event from your past, and suddenly you feel angry.

Anger is both internal and external, meaning that those around you are affected by it in the same way you are. Anger can hurt others, but will often hurt you, too.

Growing up, I struggled to identify my source of anger; to be honest, I didn't even realize I was angry or had a problem until others began to point it out. Adults and peers alike intentionally avoided me, which caused me to spend a lot of time alone. I had friends, but I realized we only clicked and got along because we were equally angry; as the saying goes "misery loves company."

I was angry all the time, woke up angry, went to bed angry. I was angry at school and at home. I knew something was off, but was not emotionally mature enough to identify my issue or its source. And the longer I stayed angry, the harder life became.

Eventually I grew tired of the loneliness and isolation and began to seek help. After several months with an awesome mentor, I could pinpoint that my issue was anger, but it was up to me to unveil the source of it. I began to ask myself important questions; was it a result of my mother's emotional (and at times physical) abuse? Was it a result of my father's unintentional absence that eventually resulted in my parents' divorce? Was it my insecurities, my environment? Bloodline? Truth be told, all of these factors have contributed to my anger, but because they remained unaddressed and unresolved for so long, each source took on a life of its own. After a while, I grew out of control, overwhelmed by the daily struggle going on inside of me.

During my anger management counseling and journey to wholeness, I learned that anger is a substitute or secondary emotion normally engaged to protect our feelings and primary emotion. Anger is an unhealthy coping and defense mechanism; it is often a cover up or mirage to our true and more vulnerable feelings. Sadness, disappointment, hurt, fear, etc. are usually the primary emotion, however, we tend to engage anger as a way to protect ourselves and keep others from seeing us in a vulnerable place or state.

The problem with anger is that it is one of the most destructive and consequential emotions; anger is one of our most intense emotional responses, and can be devastating if we are not careful. Anger can manifest for years and camouflage the real issues and problems we are holding onto. Anger can breed resentment, unforgiveness, self-hate and a host of other shattering manifestations and outcomes.

The great news, sisters, is that you don't have to stay there. There is relief, there is release and there is help! It will require your commitment, hard work and focus. You will cry, you will want to revert to old ways, you'll want to lash out, but I promise you the journey will be rewarding and life changing.

For me, there were several key steps toward my healing. I had to Admit, Uncover, Uproot and lastly Unlock. Many people turn to church or anger management counseling for assistance, and that is a great place to start. Like any counseling or intervention, the first step toward recovery is admitting that you have a problem. It is a process, and it will take time to resolve. Once you've acknowledged your anger issue, you must then take the time to carefully uncover and unveil the root and source of the problem. Consider every experience, every event, every relationship, friendship, etc. Don't discount anything, because you'd be surprised how the smallest thing can or has contributed to your anger.

Once you've uncovered the source, you must now uproot it, and that, my sister, is one of the hardest things to do. You'll cry a lot, you'll experience the pain, frustration and disappointment you did when it first happened, but it is all a part of the process, and it will bring you one step closer to complete healing. Lastly, once you've uprooted those things that can be attributed to your anger, you must unlock *new ways* of coping and dealing with circumstances, tragedies and experiences that lead to anger. Unlock positive feelings; unlock your untapped potential. Begin to invest in yourself in ways you've never done before. Develop healthy communication and coping skills; begin journaling your feelings, begin to talk through things when they happen (as opposed to letting them fester) and I promise you'll see a change. The worst thing you can do is revert to old habits and let the anger pile up and go unaddressed.

Spend time around positive people, ingest positive

imagery and speak positivity only. Develop affirmations of self-love that you can recite daily until it becomes embedded in your thinking. These things may seem tedious, but they have lasting results that are impactful and vital to your overall personal health and development.

You don't have to be angry anymore, you can change today!

SECTION II: INFINITY

Reaching

Limitlessness

CHAPTER SIX

Faux

Standards:

What We Say vs. What We Allow

Dear Sister,

If you're anything like me, establishing standards was an uncommon practice among the women in your family. Taking a look at my family tree, I identify aunts and older cousins who were in common law marriages, divorced or dealing with domestic abuse in the home. As a young girl, this was the norm in my family, neighborhood and seemingly in our culture, so I never viewed it as negative or as abnormal. However, as I grew a bit older and began to experience life outside of my home, neighborhood and circle of friends, I was exposed to other relationships, *positive* relationships, that involved sharing, healthy dialogue, respect, boundaries and authentic care for one another. I was puzzled; how were these relationships, usually involving my white counterparts, so different than the relationships I was use to observing? I grew extremely curious about the matter. From my vantage point, my aunts and older cousins were equally beautiful, intelligent and successful, yet their relationships with the opposite sex did not reflect the same level of confidence and pride I recognized when it came to their appearance, disposition toward others or their careers. What was it about the men in their lives that stripped such seemingly strong women of their confidence, leading them to tolerate cheating, disloyalty, dishonesty and such disrespect? They didn't put up with nonsense from anyone else, it seemed, so why from their men? I became so baffled that I grew frustrated. No matter how I looked at it, I just couldn't understand. And so I decided to take my genuine curiosity to the one person in my family who seemed to always have all the answers: my grandmother. In her best attempt to answer my questions and address my concerns on a level that I would comprehend and retain, she simply said "It is not a matter of the heart (love) baby girl, but the absence of enforced standards." Captivated by her wisdom, it was as if the words dropped out of her mouth in slow motion, hitting me in the chest one at a time. I was stunned by what she had identified as the problem or reason behind their ability to tolerate such disorder in their relationships and marriages.

I played my grandmother's words over and over in my mind for weeks, dissecting and examining each word one at a time until it made complete sense to me. I realized my grandmother did not say "the absence of standards," but rather "the absence of *enforced* standards." That word "enforced" is very key in her statement. How often do we proclaim to have standards, values, morals, etc. but are selective as to with whom and when they are enforced? It was then, at the tender age of thirteen, that I learned the difference between what you say vs. what you allow.

As depicted in my story above, I learned very young that the lack of standards is not always our issue, but rather that we choose not to enforce them. And this is what Magenta Women label as "Faux Standards": having a set of principles, standards and expectations, but forfeiting them to fit into someone's ideals, box or relationship.

Let's first define "standards", and then we can identity the difference between authentic and faux standards. According to Merriam-Webster, standards are defined as something established by authority, custom or general consent as a model or example. I find this definition particularly interesting, because we are the authority, my sister, that decides what behaviors, patterns, values, etc. will be allowed in our space, and which ones are simply not allowed. That is the definition of our authentic standards. But the question is: will we really require these, or instead allow them to be watered down by the lack of our enforcement?

Like a faux designer purse or faux leather jacket, faux standards are the knock-off version, imitation or counterfeit of the real thing. Faux products are but mere replicas, and because of their close resemblance, they are often hard to detect initially. However, after careful examination and a closer look, the naked eye can usually spot a fake.

Let's look at faux designer purses; they are usually decent and trendy, but are more affordable and accessible to any and every one, whereas an authentic, high-end purse is expensive and, even when on sale, it is likely you'll pay a steep price for its label and quality. And honestly, we usually don't mind paying full price for what we really want, because we know the value and quality of the item is worth every penny. Are you following me?

Anyone who knows me knows I love to shop, and one of my favorite places to shop is Nordstrom. If you've ever been in a Nordstrom, particularly the purse department, then you know all the high-end, expensive purses are always kept in glass or plastic showcases only accessible to employees who hold a key. The purses are always positioned where just about any and every customer can view them through the glass display, but only those customers who are serious about making a purchase (an investment in the expensive purse) will be granted access and invited to take a closer look.

On the other hand, if I visit the local flea market and come across counterfeit or faux purses, they are normally kept in a big bin or tub, accessible to anyone to be picked up, tried on, examined, touched etc., all before a purchase decision has been reached. How valuable and desirable is the purse if everyone has had an opportunity to touch it, grab it, try it on, take a selfie with it and then decide it's not the bag for them? The next consumer to come along will not be as inclined to even look at the bag considering how many dirty hands have held it and how many others have already tried it on without having to make the investment or purchase.

Should that not be our same approach in terms of standards set for ourselves in dating, relationships, friendships etc.? Are we not more valuable than a handbag or purse? What do we say about ourselves when any and everyone has access to us in the most intimate way, with no regard or consideration for our feelings? What does that do to our value? Stay with me and we will unveil the results of faux standards and how we establish and enforce *authentic* standards.

UNPOPULAR STANDARDS

Several years ago, I wrote a blog entry entitled "Year of the Jump-off". It was during the height of reality TV and the beginning of a culture shift where labels and terms like "jump-off" and "side chick" were introduced and embraced by pop culture and social media. As I understood it, these were terms for the mistress of a married man or of a man in a committed, public and exclusive relationship. The side chick positioned herself to entertain a three-way relationship, only the "main chick", as they call it, was unaware. Telling my age just a bit, I can remember a time when being the mistress or the other woman was frowned upon and shameful in our culture. If you were caught in an affair with a married man, caught cheating with a "spoken for man", then you were surely chastised, cast out and disregarded by friends, family and church folk. Yet we find ourselves in a time and era where it is not only *embraced*, but *celebrated*. I am no fan of reality TV, *however*, I indulge from time to time for material, and in doing so, I can't understand how such derogatory labels can be embraced by our culture. What bothers me most about this stigma is the number of beautiful sisters that are comfortable and proud to play this role in a man's life. Do we not consider the pain it causes the other woman? Are we not concerned with how devastating it is to a fellow sister? Why do we even engage in a relationship with married or committed men? How terrible it must be for both women. Now, before you ask "Why are both women hurt by this?", let's consider the external influences that may have led the "side chick" to accept her role. Taking the man completely out of the equation for just for a moment, let's focus on the role and responsibilities of the ladies involved. First you have the girlfriend or wife, to whom we refer to as the "main chick"; do you feel her standards are enforced in her relationship? I am not at all blaming her for the cheating she has endured, however, I can't be the only person who wonders if there were signs. Men will do what we allow, and won't consider what we've said. It is up to us to enforce our standards on the front end, making it clear to our partner that we won't stick around for, tolerate or put up with anything less. Does she not value herself or love herself enough to not knowingly enter into such a relationship or agreement? Does this sister not realize she is indeed worthy of genuine, uninhibited, faithful, "nobody but mine" kind of love? Now, before you judge, take a minute to reflect; we all know women in both roles, and if we're honest with ourselves, at one time or another we have played one or both roles in a relationship.

The message being sent to our women is that "standards are unpopular!" We see it all the time in memes, posts, comments etc., in stories where women have been in a relationship with a man for five, eight, ten years with no real commitment, and people make comments like "She's a ride or die chick." But I can't help but ask, is that loyalty or stupidity? How many times have you sat with your girlfriends, cousins, sister-girls and swapped stories about the foolery you've dealt with or are dealing with in a relationship? We have to move from *discussing* the problem to *resolving* the problem. And believe me when I tell you your standards (or lack thereof) are at the root of the problem.

BE THE STANDARD

I work for a Fortune 50 technology company and one of the biggest audits we approach with an "all hands on deck" strategy is our "quality standards and compliance" audit. This is when a public accounting firm sends in approximately 10-12 auditors to review our financial statements, operations and business processes to ensure we are meeting the quality standards required for our products and solutions. Should the auditors uncover any risks, even if in just one business vertical, the entire multi-billion dollar organization is considered incompliant. The effects of such audit results can be devastating and detrimental. We know that compliance is everyone's responsibility in the organization, and we all play a role in ensuring we don't put our company at risk, because we ourselves are at risk for unemployment as a result. When you consider what is at stake, what can be lost, what can be damaged or compromised, you are more likely to comply and less likely to risk losing everything you've worked for.

This is the approach we should take when enforcing our standards. It's not enough for us to set standards and vocalize them, but we have to BE the standard and truly *enforce* them. If we respect our own standards it is much more likely that the people in our lives will also respect them.

CHAPTER SEVEN

My Selfie Not Myself:

Picture Worth A Thousand Words

Dear Sister,

According to an article on Edelman.com, "We live in a time where people are consumed by entertainment. We watch it, view it, post about it, comment on it, share it, like it, follow it, tweet it, retweet and double tap/heart it for approximately 5 hours a day." Our social engagement has shifted from in-person interaction to relying solely on social media platforms and apps to assist us with dating, cooking, raising our children, earning a degree, training for a marathon and even buying a home. We have become addicted to, distracted by and obsessed with visual communication via social media platforms and apps. We want to know and want others to know where we are, what we're doing, who's with us, who we think we are and who we hope is watching.

Stylecaster.com reports that there are approximately 77.6 million US Instagram users, and that collectively we post over one million selfies a day. What's even more interesting is that approximately 36 percent of folks admitted to retouching and filtering their selfies before posting, and another 13 percent of women said they retouch every single selfie they post. Are these stats a result of an obsessive nature to be seen as perfect or to post what we wish we actually looked like? Considering that filters only enhance our natural look, why are we so hesitant to post natural, unretouched, unfiltered photos?

If I'm honest with myself and with you, I am guilty of this somewhat vain habit. Like anyone I love posting a good selfie. I have to ensure the lighting is right, my beat is on-point, my hair has no flyaways, nothing is in my nose etc., and will snap ten to fifteen pictures with the same pose, same facial expression and same look until I feel I've successfully taken the perfect selfie. And even then, I am prompted to select the filter that would present my photo in the closest to perfect way. Somehow, I have subconsciously convinced myself that I must post a perfect selfie that will result in likes, hearts, thumbs up and essentially the approval and acceptance of others. Is this a social media issue or a me issue?

Social media is merely a public platform and conduit by which we hide and mask our insecurities. It has provided a space for us to present only those things we want people to see and believe about us. It's become a grandstand to showcase and boast about what we're doing, how often we're doing it, who's hating on us getting it done and how much we don't care about what others think, when we *do* care what others think, and this is what prompts us to overindulge. Now, don't misunderstand what I mean; there is a fine line between presenting an authentic you and overexposing and oversharing on social media. However, I am focusing on the challenge women often face with self-acceptance.

This recent culture shift, social media craze and development of new social norms has convinced us that it's no longer acceptable to be your authentic self. You must look a certain way, dress a certain way and live a certain lifestyle to be "worthy". We equate Instagram hearts to love, and Facebook likes to acceptance. We even refer to followers as "friends". We are convinced that if you have a certain number of followers you are significant, popular or important. However, 9 times out 10 the same people following you are just as broken, just as insecure and just as empty. They have become dependent upon the false sense of authentication that social media provides.

We are all searching for love, validation and acceptance, but it has to start from within. I have overheard conversations between girls who have admitted "I'm going to remove my last selfie because I didn't get enough likes." Hearing statements such as these break my heart, because the cry for attention is so loud, yet none of us seem to hear it. The emptiness we feel has been overshadowed by our insatiable desire to post! Social media has become the drug we use to numb the pain associated with hurt, low self-esteem, emptiness and unforgiveness. We hide behind our posts hoping no one can see the real us, and that no one will *expose* the real us. But social media is a place where you can be anybody, so why not just be yourself?

PRACTICE WHAT YOU POST

Whether it's Facebook, SnapChat, Twitter, Instagram, or Periscope, social media has provided a stage for anyone to post whatever they desire. Everything from pictures to videos, facts to opinions, personal posts to viral videos; you can access or share just about any and everything on social media. And because of this fact, you have every right to be you! Unapologetically YOU!

My mom used to always tell me, "It is easy to pretend to be someone you're not, but it takes courage to be yourself." I challenge you to be yourself. Moving forward, share what you like, but make sure it's truly coming from you, not based on how others feel, what they think or what they may say. You'd surprised just how many people out there will find the courage to do the same, simply because you were not afraid to be you.

We live in such a diverse world and have a pretty accepting culture, so why not take advantage of such a platform to show the world just who you are? There are people out there that you are called to reach, to encourage, to motivate and to inspire. How will they ever recognize you if you are not yourself?

We hear the testimonies of celebrities all the time; if it were not for their favorite singer, actor, comedian, entertainer on television being their authentic selves, they would have never thought they too could pursue their dreams. You may not be a celebrity, you may never be on television, but I can promise you someone is watching your life and will take their cue from you. What you choose to do is indeed just that, your choice, but I know there is no one else in this world I'd rather be than me.

LOVE THY SELFIE

It's ok to love you! To unapologetically love every freckle, every wrinkle, every grey hair, crooked tooth, every imperfection and every flaw! You were wonderfully made and designed with purpose, and you must learn to love yourself. There is no filter to place on life, therefore you must embrace every part of who you are. Be so comfortable in your skin that you inspire other women to be themselves without defense or shame. I know we live in a world that tells us we have to augment and modify who we are but I'm telling you the contrary. Love exactly who you are as you are. We were not made to look the same, be the same or act the same. It's in our individuality and uniqueness that others are drawn and attracted to us.

We can't continue to risk our health, our integrity, morals and standards to be accepted by others. When I finally learned to embrace me and love myself, I noticed doing so had two responses from those around me: my bold attitude, unfiltered self-love and genuine confidence intimated some and inspired others, because women who are not afraid to be who they are can be intimidating to those who are still "faking it" or hiding behind a fierce beat, expensive purse and counterfeit posts. In the same way, women who are fearless and authentically themselves empower others to take their masks off, to embrace themselves and, in turn, to go out and do the same.

The greatest love is self-love. There is no greater reward in life than the satisfaction of completely and totally loving you! Maybe you didn't receive the validation and affirmation that was needed as a young girl. But the good news is that now you can take over the job and give yourself the love, nurture, and validation that you are seeking. You will come up short if you attempt to find it anywhere but inside of you where it always was. So, to my sister reading this book, no matter who has hurt you, has failed to appreciate you or called you ugly, unworthy or undeserving, the best response is to love thy selfie!

CHAPTER EIGHT

Compact

Mirror:

Magnifying Your Significance

Dear Sister,

My favorite compact mirror is the MAC dual image make-up mirror. It is black, sleek and fits into any purse or clutch I carry, allowing me to always be able to check my face. What I love most about my pocket mirror is how meticulously crafted and engineered it is; the mirrors are the exact same size on both sides, however, one mirror magnifies your image while the other reflects your exact image. This is not new or innovative technology, but is well-crafted nonetheless. Looking at this compact mirror from a life perspective, that is exactly how we view ourselves; we tend to magnify our flaws, imperfections and those things we identify as negative in our lives, yet we simply see from a standard vantage point the wonderful things about us. We tend to downplay the positive things because we unintentionally magnify the negative. If we are to match our inner beauty with our outer beauty, we have to shift this perspective of ourselves. We must see ourselves the way God sees us and recognize that every part of us is amazing!

REFLECTION & SELF ACTUALIZATION

Growing up insecure, one of the hardest things I've ever had to do was look at myself. (I mean *really* look at myself.) It was a combination of fear and the inability to accept who I was. I had so many internal issues that manifested externally that I struggled to even look in the mirror. As a result of this, I abandoned healthy grooming habits and put zero effort into my appearance, which later caused a down spiral and offset other issues. I avoided mirrors, and so I didn't comb my hair, I didn't invest in my appearance and would wear whatever was clean, and I just didn't care how I looked. This behavior prompted my peers to tease and bully me, which only fed the insecurities that caused me to avoid mirrors in the first place. It became a vicious cycle of self-abuse, and it was devastating to witness. When my acne became very severe, my mom took me to a dermatologist; this was the first time in several months I was forced to look at myself. Horrified by what I saw; all I could do was cry. I couldn't recognize myself anymore. It hurt me to see myself looking so unhealthy and so unhappy. I didn't realize then what we feel on the inside can affect what we look like on the outside, and that what we battle internally is certainly visible externally.

Very much like a mirror, our internal challenges and issues reflect externally. People around us can see exactly what we battle and what we fight on the inside. They may not be able to label or identify it in words, but most can see that we are hurting. What we look like is indeed a reflection of how we feel.

DUAL IMAGE SYNDROME

What is a dual image syndrome? I'm so glad you asked! Women (and men) that struggle with dual image syndrome battle with who they used to be and who are they are now. I was raised in an urban neighborhood and let's just say that although it wasn't as bad as some urban neighborhoods, it wasn't the greatest, either. I worked hard to break stereotypes and live above the stigmas and limitations that had been placed on youth and young adults raised in such areas. I worked hard in school, took a job at a young age and tried to surround myself with positive, influential and diverse people, rich in culture and on the fast track to success. What I dealt with as a result (even in my own family) were negative comments and backlash. I was accused of trying to be someone I wasn't. "What an unfair thing to say," I would think to myself, but I couldn't help but wonder if they were right. It wasn't until I reached adulthood that I grew tired of trying to lead a dual life. When with colleagues, classmates and peers that shared my same lifestyle interests I would behave one way, but the minute I was around old friends, family or people that came from the same neighborhood as me, I would revert to old ways and refrain from "acting" or being the person I worked hard to become. I finally had enough and decided I was done leading two lives. I became empowered to just be who I was regardless of what others thought. I realized *I* wasn't the problem, but those *judging me* were. I refused to apologize for the person I had become. And you shouldn't have to, either. There is a dope Jhene Aiko song lyric that says, "Shame on me for changing. No, no. Shame on you for staying the same." In the sentiment of this lyric, don't ever apologize for our evolution. Growth is life.

Being proud of who are and who you've worked hard to become should not pose a threat to others. Trying to lead a double life is just as shameful as trying to be in two relationships; it's close to impossible, and someone always gets hurt. In this case, you are the one who suffers. You deciding to change is not an indication that you don't appreciate where you've come from. Instead, it sends the message that where you started is not necessarily indicative of where you will ultimately end up. I'm grateful for my experiences; I learned a lot from my surroundings. However, I didn't learn them to stay there, but rather to come out and do even greater things.

Being proud of where you are and who you are now does not mean you are ashamed of who you used to be or where you come from. It is instead a testimony that any and everyone can be better and become greater.

CHAPTER NINE

Boss Up:

Taking Charge: Effectively Managing Your Life

Dear Sister,

BOSS MENTALITY

"Boss Up!" "Be a Boss" and "Boss Women" are phrases I hear often and see almost daily on a meme or post. Female celebrities (from Beyoncé to K. Michelle and everyone in between) have adopted this statement and made it as popular as they are. Although the word or title of a boss is nothing new to our vocabulary, it has become a staple phrase in pop culture, and has taken on a whole new meaning. So what does it truly mean to be a "boss"?

While conducting some research I looked to multiple urban dictionaries for its meaning, and of course had to refer to our traditional Merriam-Webster dictionary as well. Shockingly enough, what I found were two totally different meanings for the same word. Our culture has confused the word "boss" with being "bossy." Bossy people are fond of giving orders and being domineering, whereas being a boss simply means a person in charge. And this is what we want for each of you. To be a Boss Woman and take charge of *your* life.

How many of us were born with natural leadership instincts and intrinsic leader qualities, but because we are female were considered "bossy"? We were also referred to as bossy if we showed any signs of strength and independence. Why is it so uncommon for women to be strong leaders? Why does our culture put such a negative stigma on female leaders, as if somehow women in power threaten or disrupt a man's position of power? I am pretty sure First Lady Michelle Obama's leadership qualities don't discount those of her husband. Yet, our culture and society tell women we have no place in leadership, and if we *do* obtain a position of leadership, that we must forfeit everything else. A man can master being a leader in business and a leader in the home, and nothing seems to be threatened or neglected as a result. Yet women can't have it all; it's one or the other.

Being a boss and leader is an intangible and intrinsic skill. I believe it's something you are born with and develop or strengthen as you mature. It's your ability to influence and empower others. It's how you treat others, how you engage with others, how you guide and how you direct. It has nothing to do with being mean, forceful or domineering but rather is reflected in the way you serve others. True Boss Women have mastered the ability to serve from the front. They have recognized that they are most powerful when they empower others. Being a boss has nothing to do with income, salary, title or status, but everything to do with mindset. True Boss Women replicate themselves and produce other Boss Women.

ARE YOU AN ALPHA FEMALE?

The Alpha Female is a strong, majestic female. She can often be intimidating to those around her, and isn't afraid to ask for what she wants. She's killing it in her career and has a solid group of friends to rely on. There's nothing quite as brilliant as a woman with confidence and ambition. It is easy however for the Alpha Female to be misunderstood by her male and female counterparts. One of the main ways that she is misunderstood is the magnitude of her strength. For some it is interpreted as her being domineering, overly competitive and a threat. To others who understand that this is not the case she may be viewed as a tower of strength who is able to be there for others but does not have need for someone to be there for her. Neither of these is true of the Alpha Female.

One thing I had to learn as an Alpha Female is that while I may be naturally strong and have an intrinsic ability to lead, my strength runs low too at times and I need to have people in my life who I can count on to be supportive and nurturing to my emotional needs too.

Too often the black women's mantra is "I'm Strong!" Don't get me wrong it is wonderful to be strong. However, it took me time to learn that true strength knows vulnerability.

It's one thing to be strong and another to be tough. The woman who is strong can endure and persist. The woman who is tough will break because her strength is rooted in a pseudo source and will give in. Are you strong or tough? Have you learned where your strength runs out and who you can rely on to be there for you?

As I talked with the many women while preparing this book, *trust* constantly came up as an issue because of many childhood and adult experiences. Often times we are aware that we need more loving and nurturing relationships but we are so afraid that they will not be there for us like others who haven't in our past. But we must make a very bold decision at some point not to let our past hold our future hostage. If you are going to be a true Boss Woman, you will need to be strong but you cannot afford to be tough. Being tough will mean that you are locked in to a place that while it is protecting, will keep you locked in and others locked out. Let's choose strength over toughness and embrace the beauty of vulnerability as a part of true strength.

"NO" IS A COMPLETE SENTENCE

Oftentimes as women with authority, we struggle with saying no. We feel obligated to be the Superwoman in everyone's life, allowing others to drain us, pull us in multiple directions, take from us and use us, sometimes without realizing it. This is why, as a Boss Woman, you must learn to say no. Your ability to say no does not rob you of your ability to lead, but rather *enhances* your ability to lead. Great leaders know they can't take every meeting, attend every engagement or be everything to everyone.

What does your ability to say no have to do with taking charge and managing your life? Everything! Your ability to say no is by far one of the most critical healthy social habits you'll develop in life. It is so easy for us to become inundated, overwhelmed and consumed by the issues, challenges and requests of others, so much so that they become *our* issues, challenges and priorities. Many of us are guilty of falling victim to the vicious cycle of putting others before ourselves, and it's not intentional, but we desire to be helpful, we desire to please, we desire to be liked and accepted, and for some of us, we simply do not know how to say no!

For years, my family and friends would call on me for just about everything. Whether borrowing money, babysitting their children, co-signing on a car…you name it, I've been asked. And not all the requests were bad (some truly were legit in that they needed to vent, wanted to advice or just wanted someone to talk to), but in those instances, it can be draining if the person has not positioned themselves to change the situation they continue to vent about. And if we are not careful, we begin to adopt and ingest the same things that have upset and discouraged them.

In my sophomore year of undergrad, one of my study buddies was in the most toxic relationship possible. Although there was no physical abuse, she was definitely being emotionally abused. Every time we came together to study, we spent the first fifty minutes of our sessions talking about her "no good, trifling, cheating boyfriend." At first I thought I was being a good friend by listening, and providing support and advice where warranted. After a while, though, I noticed every time I talked to her I would have an attitude or uneasy feeling afterward. There were days I would even be upset with my own boyfriend, and could not find a valid reason as to why he and I were beefing. It took the following event to finally realize I had to tell her NO and put some boundaries in place. We were on the phone discussing a recent exam and sharing our results. About halfway through the call she somehow worked her boyfriend into the conversation. Her rant and complaining went on for about 35 minutes. All of a sudden my ear was literally burning. At first I thought it may have been a result of my earring and cell phone being pressed against each other. However, days after the call, my ear was still hurting. I went to urgent care and learned that I had an ear infection in my left ear. Now, call me crazy, but I surely blamed that toxic conversation on my sudden ear infection. I believe that infection was a physical representation of what was taking place inside me every time we spoke and she dumped her toxic words into my spirit. It took the physical infection for me to identify the emotional and spiritual infection that had been forming hence my uneasy feeling after each conversation. Something had to change. So I invited her to meet and politely shared that we could no longer talk about her relationship if she was not willing to change it.

I learned from that situation that although I meant well, I couldn't allow others to drain or contaminate me; it's impossible for us to effectively serve others if we ourselves are empty. Self-preservation and self-care are vital to our personal growth and sustainability. There are dozens of memes and quotes that carry the saying "people who love the hardest are often hurt the most." However, I have to turn the mirrors in and take a look at why this has become such a fact.

FINDING BALANCE

My business partner and I are indeed "Boss Women!" We are both self-motivated, driven and dedicated to pursuing a full and rewarding life. We are business minded, professionally mature and goal-oriented. These all seem to be great likenesses, however, we are both guilty in lacking balance at times. We pursue our dreams at any cost, even if it means we work until exhaustion. We recently committed to being deliberate in building a more harmonious life. This doesn't mean we have to forfeit or abort any of our dreams and ambitions, but rather that we must find a way to lead healthy lives where everything flows together in harmony. Finding time to date, time with family and just time for ourselves is critical. We recognize just how important this is, and want to share some of these tips with you our Magenta Ladies.

Establishing harmony is essential to your personal development and professional success. Effectively managing your life has to include "me-time". It is imperative to enforce self-care and self-perseveration; not only are they foundational elements of self-love, but they are vital in leading a full-life. There is no point in acquiring wealth, reaching success and never actually getting a chance to enjoy life.

Building a harmonious life has to be intentional and deliberate. Schedule a day or two that you take no work calls, no appointments and no meetings. Use those days to do something for yourself. Go to a movie, attend a show, take a staycation or a night out with the girls.

I'll admit, as a boss and workaholic it can be difficult to do nice things for yourself. We put everyone and everything first, and often feel guilty for taking time out for ourselves. But I promise if you take the first step toward harmony, it *will* get easier, and you *will* be able to do so on a consistent basis. It's great to lead others, but you must first master leading yourself. The most effective leaders lead by example.

One of the biggest factors that has helped me in my journey of creating more harmony is being realistic about my current space and what I can *actually* get done. Often times if we can be honest we simply have bitten off more than we can chew and we are wondering why pieces of our lives are falling apart at the seams.

I live off of a block calendar system and highly encourage it for you ladies. I take a 7 day 24 hour calendar and I fill it with my activities. There is a catch though. I start with my highest priorities and work down. So I start with my spirit, when in the week will I connect with God and take care of myself spiritually. Then I add in me time. Yes me-time is second. When in the week will I take care of myself? When will I get rest, pamper myself, read and do things I need just for me? I actually plug these items into the calendar. And I continue on down the list with family time, girlfriend time, career, etc. And once the calendar is full, it is full. If there are activities that didn't make it on the calendar now I must really take a moment to decide if it is important enough to replace something else that is currently on the calendar. If not then this is an indicator that for this current season of my life that activity is not in harmony and I cannot participate no matter how strongly I desire to.

I know this can be difficult but I had to realize that I cannot let fear and anxiety run my time. The truth is my sister sometimes we run ourselves in the ground because of this underlying fear that we can't get it all done or that we are behind where we should be when the truth is when we learn to relax we realize that we are exactly where God needs us to be at this juncture of time. Everything that we are assigned to do in this life we will be able to do. We do not need to attempt to jumble it all together and run ourselves in the ground. Get done in this season of life what you have the capacity to do and once you maximize *this* moment, you will be ready to elevate to the next.

You will find much more balance and life harmony my sister when you find the flow and rhythm of life set by God and live daily to that cadence. Harmony is yours for the taking. Will you create it?

CHAPTER TEN

Role Call:

Who's On Your Team?

Dear Sister,

IDENTIFYING TOXIC RELATIONSHIPS

Your spectators, your haters and your supporters all have the same view of your life; how they choose to respond to your blessings and your success will confirm the role they play.

Take a good look at your current circle; really examine your inventory of friends. Now place them into the following categories: my motivators, my accountability partners and my supporters. Did everyone you identify fit into at least one of these categories? No? Ok, let's look again, and now tell me if anyone in your circle can fall into one of these categories: the needy, the negative or the neglectful. These are much harder categories to sort and filter, but we have to be completely subjective and honest. We all have people in our lives that can fit into at least one of those secondary categories, but for the sake of clarity, let's take a closer look at each role.

Motivators: These are your friends that always push you to be your greatest self. They will often remind you of the goals and dreams you've set for yourself, and will often motivate you to continue pursuing them diligently.

Accountability Partners: Sometimes your accountability partners can also be motivators, however, they will take their role as friends to the next level. Accountability partners will not allow you to fall and stay down; they will hold you to your word and not allow you to give up. If you experienced a recent break-up and asked this friend to make sure you don't give in to his numerous request to still see or contact you, you better believe your accountability partner is going to be sure you keep far away from the ex!

Supporters: I'm sure you're thinking, "What's the difference between motivators and supporters?" but you'd be surprised; supporters are those friends that will be at every event you host, every speaking engagement you have, the family functions you invite them to etc. Any and everything that's important to you will be important to them. Supporters celebrate you and your achievements as if they were their own. Supporters may not always push you to pursue your dreams and goals, but are usually in the front row cheering for you when you do.

For every motivator, accountability partner and supporter in our circle, you can be certain many of us have needy, negative and neglectful friends. (I'm pretty confident you will identify at least one among you.) Let's take a quick look at the characteristics and attributes of such fakes among friends.

The Needy: Needy people tend to always attach themselves to the driven, the motivated, the successful, the caring, the givers and the emotionally mature. It's usually because they recognize in others what they themselves are lacking personally. Most needy people aren't even aware of their "leech like ways", and so are never intentional in their clingy, needy and smothering behavior. They simply are not in a position to deposit into you to the degree they withdraw from you. Needy friends can come across as admirers or fans, but if you're not careful can be draining and leave you feeling depleted.

The Negative: These are by far the most dangerous to invite in your circle, and are even worse once they become comfortable in your personal space. Negative people usually have no regard for others and are dream killers, blockers or de-motivators. Like the needy, negative people don't always mean you harm, but because of their own unhappiness, shortcomings, brokenness etc., their negative views and perspectives concerning their own life can spill over into yours. One of the most difficult things to recognize in negative people is the root of their negativity and how it can affect you and your friendship long term.

The Neglectful: Now, I know a lot about this type of friend, because sadly, I used to be one. Neglectful friends are by far the hardest to recognize in your circle. They are often present, but are not supportive or motivating. Again, unintentionally, they are usually preoccupied with their own issues, challenges, goals or agenda. Neglectful friends will only engage if you are the one to reach out first, but will allow you to go months without speaking or connecting unless you make the first move. These type of friends are usually just as self-motivated but are a bit more selfish; they focus solely on themselves, what they have going on and what's important to them. Here's an example: you call your friend to see how they are, just to connect and converse because it's been some time since you've been in touch. As soon as you ask "how have you been?" they go on and on for close to twenty minutes without even once asking how you are. Neglectful friends are convinced nothing and no one is as important as what they have going on personally.

ATTACHMENT VS. CONNECTION

When I think attachment I think of two things that are linked together at the surface level. Versus when two things are connected, they have been intertwined in some way. So it can be in our relationships. We can have friends that we have a surface level connection with but there is no true connection. It is important to note that sometimes we can attach to people for the wrong reasons. Sometimes it is our brokenness that attaches us to a person. Maybe we both have low self-esteem. Or possibly we both have body-image issues and we relate on that level. Examine your friendships for a moment and reflect on the level of relationship. Are you attached (at the surface level) or is there a true connection (deeper intertwining).

When you are truly connected to someone there is a part of them in you and a part of the you in them. Don't get me wrong they will not be a carbon copy of you. It took me a minute to really truly get that. I would be closer to my friends who were seemingly just like me, almost twins, and not as close to the ones who didn't necessarily dress like me, behave like me but we still had plenty in common. I had to learn though to appreciate the differences in my relationships but still value the connection.

Where there is an attachment it can be easily broken whereas something that is truly connected cannot be easily separated. I encourage you to fortify your life with true meaningful connection friendships versus surface level attachments that may not be structured to be sustained long-term.

THE ELIMINATION ROUND – WHEN IT'S TIME TO LET GO

I met my best friend at 15 years old. We knew immediately we'd be inseparable, and that we would experience every significant milestone as besties. We traveled together, went to school together, worked together, and she even dated my brother. At some point, she transitioned from friend to family. I would do anything for her and loved having her in my life. It felt so great to have a best friend, someone who could identify and relate, someone who I felt didn't judge and would never disappoint me. As we grew older and began to pursue separate interests, I noticed a shift in our friendship but thought nothing of it. We were headed in two very different directions, and yet I refused to accept that we were not as close as we once were. Afraid to lose my friend, I tried to convince myself that I was tripping, and that things were the same. However, after a while, things were blatantly clear that we were different and wanted very different things out of life; I was making plans to attend college, and she was going on with life as usual, no plans, no ambition, and no pursuit of life outside her parents' home. I was puzzled and would often check myself. "Maybe you're judging her; maybe you're being too hard on her."

For years I forced a friendship that just didn't exist anymore. I refused to let go. In my eyes, she hadn't betrayed me, hadn't done anything wrong, was still trustworthy and loyal, so why did I have to let her go as a friend? It wasn't until she finally pulled away from me that I realized this was something I should have done years prior.

Many of you can relate; how many people in your life are good people but you are no longer connected? This can be applied to friendships or relationships. We try so hard to hold onto what was, know deep down in our hearts there is no mutual benefit in holding on. In any friendship or relationship there should be an exchange. You should both be in a position to support and encourage one another. Growing up does not always mean growing apart if the friendship is authentic. However, when it's not, we must be honest with ourselves and position ourselves to let go and move on.

OPEN CASTING: NETWORKING

I am a firm believer in "your network determines your networth." Your connections, your network and your circle are key contributors to your overall success and trajectory as a professional and individual. *Who* you know directly supports *what* you know, and *what* you have access to. Being connected to the right people or being affiliated with the right organizations should be a part of everyone's overall success plan. Needless to say, networking is one of the most underutilized free development tools out there. Networking costs nothing, yet many people fail to make the investment. Is it fear of being rejected or dismissed? Or is simply lack of know how?

Whether attempting to build a brand or a business, start an organization or to land your ideal job, here a few tips that may aid you in developing networking skills that will warrant immediate and lasting relationships.

First take the pressure off. So often when I see people networking they are like dogs in heat hoping that each person they meet is their next client or their big break. They behave like the desperate girl who is trying to determine from the first date if this guy could be the one. Too soon. Relax! As you network simply enjoy meeting people. I have learned that relationships can blossom and become something I genuinely never expected but it takes time. There are so many people who I connected with and stayed connected to and nurtured the connection only for the true purpose of our paths crossing to show up much later. I shudder to think what I would have missed out on if I had dismissed them early because I couldn't see it or if I came across to eager. When we learn to relax and enjoy meeting people we will be able to attract more quality people into our space.

Next, be selfless in networking. I am I the only one who can't stand being at an event and having bum rush me with their card and bombard me with all the great things they are doing but they take no genuine interest in what I am doing. No thank you! I have learned the true secret sauce of networking is leading with a listen. I intentionally start networking conversations by asking questions and learning more about the person. What am I listening for? The hook, the connection, to see if there is any. Sometimes we give everyone our perfectly rehearsed script without even qualifying if this is someone we should say that to. Not every person will be a connection or someone we are meant to stay in contact with. I listen for key things that let me know there is a mutual benefit to us being connected. Minus that I will keep the conversation light. Be intentional about networking my sister. It is not about the quantity, but rather the quality of your network.

BUILDING RELATIONSHIPS THAT NURTURE

With all things considered on the matter, I challenge you to take action and commit to immediate changes in terms of the relationships you invest in. Be deliberate in pursuing, building and fostering healthy relationships. Identify friends, affiliates, contacts, mentors and even potential mates that will nurture, support, motivate and inspire you. Invest in relationships that will furnish ROI (a return on your investment). I know that may sound like a business transaction or business agreement, however, we should approach friendships and relationships the same way we pursue business in terms of expectations, standards and goals.

If your goal is to date, be sure to date with purpose and know exactly what you want before you engage or get involved. If it's lasting friendships you seek, connect with other women who have similar goals and interests. If nothing else, just be the type of friend you desire and good things will come to you.

The Charge:

Don't Let Your Crown Fall

Dear Sister,

According to Wikipedia "a crown worn by a Queen represents power, legitimacy, righteousness, victory, triumph, honor and glory." In the game of chess, the Queen is the most powerful piece; she can move any number of squares and in any direction. In the United Kingdom the Queen is the head of state, ruler, decision maker, and the most revered. In a deck of cards, the Queen is among the most valuable face cards in a winning hand known as a the "Royal Flush." The Queen Bee (not a reference to Beyonce) is the mother of most if not all and is the most important bee in her colony or hive. These Queens that I've just identified know their positions and never forfeit their place or compromise their title. They are Queens all day every day. Their behavior, words, actions, thoughts, habits, etc. all reflect that of a

Queen. In the same way you my dear sister are important, valuable, and significant and yes you too are a Queen! Your invisible crown should adorn your head daily and be a constant reminder of the life you deserve, the treatment you are worthy of, the love you should receive and the mannerism you should display.

Notice that I said "don't let your crown fall" not "don't drop your crown!" I was intentional in my choice of words because I want to illustrate that we are not always responsible for the things that happen to us and there will be circumstances and situations in life that will threaten the position of our crowns or even cause them to fall.

10% of life is what happens to us, the other 90% is how we *choose* to respond. At times, things are out of our control and can bear devastating results that impact our self-esteem, self-love, trust and motivation; however, know that you have the power to seize anything that would attempt to pollute your spirit, contaminate your thinking, violate your morals, degrade your body, discredit your character, damage your self-esteem or discount your worth! You ARE a Queen and are worthy of your crown. You are not required to earn it, prove that you deserve it or wait for others to acknowledge it. It is yours and do not let anyone take it, borrow it or convince you to take it off.

Know that what you offer the world cannot be purchased and is truly priceless. Every idea, every gift, every talent... everything down to your smile is unique to you and was uniquely and wonderfully made by God. Affirm daily that you are a Queen! Remind yourself as often as you need to that you are priceless, worthy of success, endless love and a limitless life!

Keep your head up my sister and keep that crown in place!

Sincerely,

Tiff & Tima

www.ingramcontent.com/pod-product-compliance
Lightning Source LLC
LaVergne TN
LVHW051600080426
835510LV00020B/3073